New York
Native Peoples

Mark Stewart

Heinemann Library
Chicago, Illinois

www.capstonepub.com
Visit our website to find out more information about Heinemann-Raintree books.

To order:

☎ Phone 800-747-4992

🖳 Visit www.capstonepub.com
to browse our catalog and order online.

©2003, 2009 Heinemann-Raintree
an imprint of Capstone Global Library
Chicago, Illinois

Editorial: Megan Cotugno
Design: Kimberly R. Miracle, Betsy Wernert, Ryan Frieson
Photo Research: Tracy Cummins
Production: Alison Parsons

Originated by Chroma Graphics Pte Ltd.
Printed and bound in the United States of America in North Mankato, Minnesota. 082012   006901

ISBN-13: 978-1-4329-1131-7 (hc)
ISBN-13: 978-1-4329-1138-6 (pb)

14 13 12
10 9 8 7 6 5 4 3 2

The Library of Congress has cataloged the first edition as follows: Stewart, Mark.
  New York Native peoples : New York State studies / Mark Stewart.
      p. cm.
  Summary: Describes the history, environment, beliefs of the Native Peoples of New York state, and the organization of the Iroquois Confederacy, and profiles some famous individuals, such as Joseph Brant and Handsome Lake.
  Includes bibliographical references and index.
  ISBN 978-1-4329-1131-7 (hc) --
  ISBN 978-1-4329-1138-6 (pb) 1. Indians of North America--New York (State)--Juvenile literature.
  [1. Indians of North America--New York (State)] I. Title.
  E78.N7S7655 2003
  974.7004'97--dc21
                                            2002154311

Acknowledgments
The author and publishers are grateful to the following for permission to reproduce copyright material:
p. 9 ©The Mariners' Museum/Corbis; **p. 10** ©Michelle Mouldenhauer/Archaeological Society of Virginia; **pp. 12, 13** ©North Wind Picture Archives; **pp. 16, 25T** ©Corbis; **pp. 18, 40** ©Marilyn Angel Wynn/Nativestock Pictures/Corbis; **pp. 23, 31** ©Marilyn "Angel" Wynn/Nativestock; **pp. 20, 21** ©John Kahionhes Fadden; **pp. 22, 33** ©The Granger Collection, NY; **p.24T** ©Geanina/Shutterstock; **p. 24B** ©Carnegie Museum of Natural History; **p. 25B** ©National Museum of the American Indian/Neg # NP/29396; **p. 27** ©General Research Division/Astor, Lenox and Tilden Foundations/New York Public Library; **p. 29** ©Rochester Museum and Science Center/MR545; **p. 30** ©Notman Photographic Archives/McCord Museum of Canadian History, Montreal; **pp. 34, 36** ©Hulton Archive/Getty Images; **p. 37** ©Library of Congress; **pp. 38, 42T** ©Buffalo & Erie County Historical Society; **p. 41** ©Rudi von Briel/Heinemann Library; **p. 42B** ©AP Wide World Photo

Cover Image reproduced with permission of ©Corbis.

The publishers would like to thank Nancy Harris for her assistance in the preparation of this book.

Disclaimer
All the Internet addresses (URLs) given in this book were valid at the time of going to press. However, due to the dynamic nature of the Internet, some addresses may have changed, or sites may have changed or ceased to exist since publication. While the author and publisher regret any inconvenience this may cause readers, no responsibility for any such changes can be accepted by either the author or the publisher.

Contents

Some words are shown in bold, **like this**. You can find out what they mean by looking in the glossary.

Prehistoric New York

The first people to live in present-day New York probably arrived about 11,000 years ago. That time is known as the last **Ice Age**. The earth's **climate** was colder than it is now, and much of North America was covered with thick, slowly moving sheets of ice called glaciers. The level of the oceans was about 300 feet (91 meters) lower, because much of the water existed as ice in glaciers. The lower water levels meant that much of the seafloor was exposed as land. Between Asia and North America, the water level dropped enough to leave a land bridge, which animals and people could move across. As the climate slowly warmed over hundreds of years, the land bridge was again covered by ocean water.

Paleo-Indian Migration

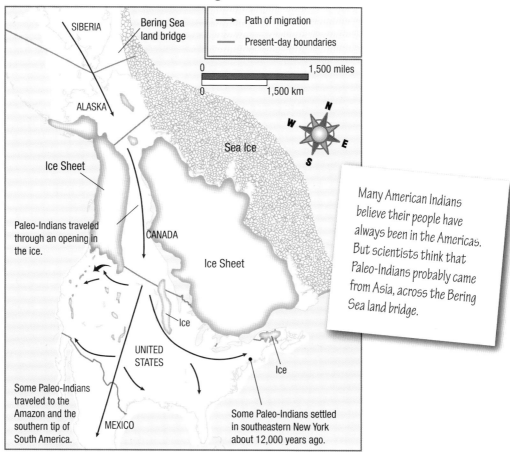

SIBERIA
Bering Sea land bridge
→ Path of migration
— Present-day boundaries

0   1,500 miles
0   1,500 km

ALASKA

Sea Ice

Ice Sheet

Paleo-Indians traveled through an opening in the ice.

CANADA

Ice Sheet

Ice

UNITED STATES

Ice

Some Paleo-Indians traveled to the Amazon and the southern tip of South America.

MEXICO

Some Paleo-Indians settled in southeastern New York about 12,000 years ago.

Many American Indians believe their people have always been in the Americas. But scientists think that Paleo-Indians probably came from Asia, across the Bering Sea land bridge.

New York's Native Peoples

Paleo-Indians	Archaic	Woodland	Historic Indians
ca. 10,000 BCE to 8000 BCE	ca. 8000 BCE to 500 BCE	ca. 500 BCE to 1500 CE	ca. 1500 CE to Present

Paleo-Indians

Scientists think that the first people to **migrate** across the land bridge from Asia to North America were Paleo-Indian hunters. Groups of Paleo-Indians followed herds of animals they depended on for food, such as the woolly mammoth. Paleo-Indians probably migrated south and east slowly over thousands of years, first arriving in New York around 10,000 BCE. Paleo-Indians hunted and gathered for survival, using stone spear points and other stone tools. They used animal skins and the **environment** around them for clothing and shelter.

Archaic Indians

The Archaic period started when the climate became warmer around 8000 BCE. By that time, plants had changed and many large animals once hunted by Paleo-Indians had become **extinct**. Indians of the Archaic period hunted deer, elk, bear, and moose. Toward the end of the Archaic period, Indians may have kept some plants in small gardens. Archaic Indians also made stone tools and carved bowls from rock.

Woodland Indians

The Woodland period began around 500 BCE. Indians of the Woodland period began to farm, which allowed them to live in more permanent villages. With a more settled life, village groups became larger. People were able to develop better tools, since they no longer had to move constantly to follow the food supply. Woodland Indians made better tools than those of the Archaic period. They began making pottery to use for cooking and storage. Since there was more food, not everyone had to **forage**, or hunt for food all the time. So, some people were free to become warriors or priests. Women had time to decorate their pottery and make jewelry. Different Woodland Indian **tribes** traded with one another.

Historic Indians

Before European settlers arrived in North America in the 1600s, there were two large groups of people living in what we now call New York. For many years, the Algonquian and Iroquois Indians occupied the vast territory stretching from the Atlantic Ocean to the Great Lakes. This included New York. They were the **descendants** of the Paleo, Archaic, and Woodland Indians. The Iroquois actually call themselves Haudenosaunee (ho-den-o-show-nee), which means "people of the longhouse." *Iroquois* is the French version of *Irinakhoiw*, the Algonquian name for the Haudenosaunee meaning "rattlesnakes." The Haudenosaunee lived throughout most of northern, central, and western New York, while the Algonquians lived near the Atlantic Ocean and along the Hudson River.

Mound Builders

Some Indians of the Woodland period were members of a mound-building people called the Hopewell. Their **culture** stretched from the Mississippi River to the Atlantic Ocean. Hopewell burial mounds have been found in western New York. The Hopewell hunted, fished, and gathered plants for food. They honored their dead and traded with their neighbors. They made things out of copper and carved stone, and grew and smoked tobacco. The Hopewell were probably the first large-scale farmers in New York. They grew large fields of corn.

The mound builders were gone long before the first European explorers arrived in the 1500s. **Archaeologists** now think that around 1,600 years ago the climate in New York became cooler, making it harder to grow corn. By that time, the mound builders had become skilled with the bow and arrow. Since they could no longer rely on corn, they found it was smarter to follow and hunt the animals for food than to stay in one place. After many centuries, the mound builders may have simply left New York as a matter of survival.

New York American Indians, ca. 1722

0 ——— 50 miles
0 ——— 50 km

N
W — E
S

Lake Champlain

Lake Ontario

Mohawk
Tuscarora
Oneida
Onondaga
Cayuga
Seneca

Lake Erie

Hudson River

Atlantic Ocean

Mohawk   Rough location of tribe
☐   Iroquois Confederacy
☐   Algonquian Indians

This map shows the nations of the Iroquois Confederacy in 1722. By that time, remaining Algonquians had been pushed into eastern New York.

The **ancestors** of the Haudenosaunee moved into New York from Pennsylvania around 900 CE. Before that, the Algonquians lived throughout the state and much of eastern and central Canada. When the two groups fought, the Algonquians were driven east past the Hudson River, into parts of present-day New York City, northern New York, and Canada. When Europeans arrived in New York, they encountered these two main groups of people who had lived here for years.

Algonquian People

When the Iroquois came into New York from the west, they found Algonquian Indians from several **tribes** already living in the area. The Algonquian people had no central organization outside their own clans and tribes, so it was difficult for them to fight off invaders as a group. But the Iroquois tribes had formed a **confederacy**, a type of organization that joined them together. The Iroquois Confederacy drove the Algonquian Indians farther east. Because of the power and organization of the Iroquois Confederacy, the Algonquian people who lived in New York and their way of life are sometimes overlooked. However, they were the first American Indians living in the land now known as New York.

Organization and Villages

Most Algonquian tribes were similar in many ways, including the organization of their villages. Villages were usually located along rivers or other large bodies of water. They were a source of fresh water for drinking and important for transportation. Travel by water was the best way to move about until the mid–1800s.

Algonquian Tribes

There were many Algonquian tribes originally living in New York. The following are just some of the best known tribes:

Lenape (or Delaware)	(le-nah-pee)
Mahican (or Mohican)	(mah-hee-kahn)
Montauk	(mahn-tawk)
Munsee (Lenape sub-tribe)	(muhn-see)
Wappinger	(wahp-ping-er)

Dugout Canoes

The dugout canoe was very important for the Algonquians. Canoes were used for travel, to carry things, and for fishing. They could be as small as 8 to 10 feet (2.4 to 3 meters) long, or large enough to carry as many as 40 people.

To make a canoe, the Indians would build a fire at the base of a wide tree trunk in order to make it fall. They would then burn out a long hole down the center of the tree trunk while also scraping the bark and wood away. The Algonquians sometimes rubbed bear fat on the smooth wood to keep it from rotting. They used wooden paddles or poles to make the canoe move.

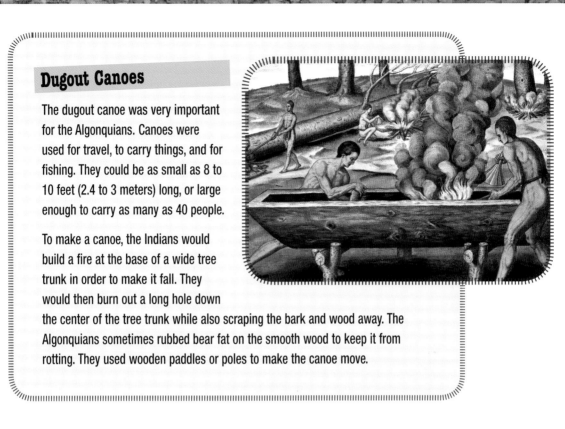

Each Algonquian village usually functioned on its own. The village was governed by two chiefs, a council of **elders**, and the residents of the village. The two chiefs included a war chief and a peace chief. The peace chief either **inherited** his position or was elected by the village. The peace chief ran meetings and **ceremonies**, directed large hunts, and settled arguments. The war chief was appointed by the people because of his skills in battle. His authority only lasted as long as a war was being fought.

Most Algonquian tribes were divided into clans, which were like large, extended family groups. Clans were usually named after an animal such as the wolf, bear, or turtle. Clan and family memberships were usually traced through the mother. This meant that a chief inherited his position through his mother, rather than through his father. It was usually expected that a person would marry someone outside his or her own clan. When a man married, he would move in with his wife's clan.

Villages of Algonquian tribes were usually not protected by a wall. However, if a village was located near an enemy tribe, it might be protected by a **palisade** made of tree trunks. Villages could have as many as 500 to 600 people.

Shelter

Algonquian villages consisted of either longhouses or *wigwams*. Both types of home were made by bending **saplings**, which are young trees, into an arch and then tying them together with string made from animal muscle or plant **fiber**. This frame was then covered completely with sheets of tree bark or woven mats made of river **reeds**. Much of the work in making the houses was done by the women. Longhouses could be from 20 to 100 feet (6 to 30.5 meters) long, and more than one family usually shared a longhouse.

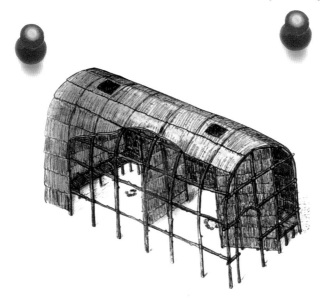

Algonquian longhouses (above) and *wigwams* (right) were very practical. They offered protection from outside weather, but could be rebuilt if the village had to move, since the materials could be easily found in the region.

Small, round houses called *wigwams* were built for summer camps and hunting trips. They were made from the same materials as longhouses, but would only hold a single family. Because of their size, *wigwams* could be easily taken apart and rebuilt, which made them ideal for temporary shelter. In both longhouses and *wigwams*, a fire was kept burning to keep away evil spirits. A hole was left in the roof over each fire to let the smoke out.

Food

The men of Algonquian tribes hunted and fished, and the women gathered food and farmed. Men hunted bear, elk, deer, beaver, muskrat, and other animals. They also hunted and trapped birds and ate their eggs. The deer was the most common and important animal hunted by most tribes. Hunters used spears made of wood with bone or stone points. They also used the bow and arrow, which became their main weapon and tool for hunting over the years.

A man usually hunted by himself. He wore the skin of a deer and could sneak right up to the deer or other animal. In the fall season, however, whole villages participated in a large hunt. In village hunts, the Indians would set fire to an area, surrounding a herd of deer. They would leave an opening in order to easily capture and kill many deer at one time. The women and girls of the village would then help prepare the deer meat. They scraped the skins, roasted and boiled some of the meat, and cut the rest of the meat into strips to be dried and made into **jerky**. The Indians used every part of the animals they hunted, letting nothing go to waste. Skins were made into clothing, and bones were made into tools.

Indian hunters dressed in deerskins could walk right up to the deer. Algonquians were expert hunters who had great respect for their prey. They could track animals very well without being seen, heard, or smelled.

Fish were another important source of food for the American Indians of New York. Men caught fish using nets, lines, or spears. They also used nets to catch shellfish such as **mussels**, clams, and oysters. The fish were either dried in the sun or **smoked**. The Lenape Indians of New York fished for shad and sturgeon using huge nets to catch hundreds at a time. Thousands of these fish swim into New York rivers from the Atlantic Ocean every spring to deposit their eggs.

Women of Algonquian tribes farmed and gathered food, and their children would often help them. Women and children gathered plants, roots, berries, fruits, mushrooms, and nuts from fields and forests. Most of this food was eaten as soon as it was ripe, but large amounts could be dried and stored for the winter. In the spring, women and children collected wild strawberries, blueberries, and blackberries. They also gathered and ate persimmons, cranberries, wild plums, and the roots of cattail plants and water lilies. Walnuts, hickory nuts, and chestnuts were gathered in October and November. Oak trees supplied many acorns. Women removed the bitter taste of the acorns by roasting or crushing them and rinsing them with hot water. The roasted or crushed acorns could be cooked in porridge or pounded into flour for bread.

Most Algonquian women planted gardens, which were sometimes large enough to be considered small farms. They planted corn, beans, and squash all together, because they help each other grow. Corn was the most important crop. Women also planted sunflowers, pumpkins, herbs, and tobacco, which was smoked in ceremonies. Most vegetables were eaten when they were ripe. Some were stored for the winter.

The manner of their fishing.

When fishing at night from canoes, it was often the job of Algonquian boys and girls to keep a fire going in the center of the canoe. The fire attracted fish toward the canoe, where they could be caught.

Clothing and Appearance

Algonquian men shaved off all of their facial hair. Women often colored their faces with red or yellow **ocher**. Both men and women commonly tattooed their bodies with animal designs. Men sometimes pierced their ears with porcupine **quills**. Tribal elders often wore their hair long, but warriors shaved the sides of their heads and had a lock of hair on top. Warriors shaved the sides of their heads so that their hair would not get caught in their bows while fighting or hunting. They often greased their lock of hair so it would stand straight up. Clothing was made from deerskins and decorated with shell beads or porcupine quills, feathers, and other ornaments.

Algonquian men often wore **breechcloths** and moccasins made from animal skin, usually from a deer. They wore leggings and a robe made with thick animal skins to keep warm in winter. Women wore long skirts made of animal skins. They wore fur robes in winter, or made an attractive **mantle** out of turkey feathers. Women also wore ornaments of bone, shell, and *wampum*, a type of shell bead, as necklaces and bracelets. The first European explorers in the New York region described the Algonquian Indians they encountered as tall, bronze in color, and gracious in manner.

This woman has the typical tattoos, skirt, and jewelry of Algonquian tribes. The decoration of the skirt and quality of the jewelry depended on a woman's status, or importance, in the tribe.

Algonquian mothers wrapped newborn children in animal skins, which were then attached to **cradleboards**. The mothers hung their cradleboards and babies on the branches of trees while they were working in their gardens. They believed the cradleboards would help their children's bones grow straight and strong. Young children who could walk wore very little other than moccasins, except in winter, when they wore robes made from animal skin, similar to the adults.

Religion and Ritual

Each Algonquian tribe of New York had its own slightly different set of beliefs and **rituals**. Every tribe believed they were a part of the natural world, which they treated with great respect. Almost all plants and animals were believed to contain spirits. A strong respect for nature was especially important since the American Indians relied on the plants, animals, and water around them for survival.

The Algonquians believed in an **afterlife**. A person's spirit or soul left the body at death and eventually traveled to the land of the spirits. The land of the spirits was a pleasant place, with plenty of good hunting, where the spirit would be reunited with relatives that had already passed on. Algonquian tribes worshiped several gods, one of which was the supreme being and creator, with the lesser gods serving him. Each tribe had its own story of how the world and its people were created.

All villages had a medicine man who could cure illnesses and talk to the spirit world. Medicine men could interpret dreams in order to predict the future. They were as important as chiefs in American Indian villages. Illness was thought to be caused by evil spirits entering the body. Medicine men used drums, rattles, **sacred herbs**, and chants to scare away evil spirits and cure the illness.

Algonquian tribes had various rituals and celebrations for different occasions and times of the year. Celebrations usually included music and dance. Gourds, river canes, turtle shells, and other items were used to make drums, rattles, and other instruments. A celebration for the fall harvest of crops was common among Algonquian tribes. Those celebrations could last as long as two weeks. Some tribes constructed a special longhouse in the center of their villages where most important ceremonies and celebrations were held.

Medicine men used age-old methods to cure a patient. This medicine man is using a sacred rattle and song to communicate with the spirits while mixing an **herbal** medicine.

Algonquian boys went through a trial of manhood, usually between the ages of 12 and 17. In order to become men and be allowed to marry, boys of a village were expected to go out and survive in the forest alone for months. They had to rely on the hunting and survival skills they learned from the men of the village. Sometimes the trial of manhood included a period of fasting, where the boys would go without food for several days. This would allow them to see visions. In such a **vision quest**, a boy might be visited by an animal spirit that would become his spirit guardian for life. Once a boy proved he could do the work of a man and went through the trial of manhood of the village, he was free to marry. Algonquian girls did not usually have to go through a trial of womanhood. An Algonquian girl was considered a woman once she could do the work of a woman well. This was sometimes as young as age 13. At that point she could marry.

Lenape Football

The Lenape Indians of New York played a game of football that involved a team of men versus a team of women. The ball was oblong in shape, made of deerskin, and stuffed with deer hair. There were goal posts on each end of a field. The ball had to make it in between the goal posts for a score. Once 12 total points were scored, the game ended. The team with the most points out of 12 won. Women players could pass the ball, run with the ball, and tackle male players. Men were only allowed to kick the ball toward their goal and knock the ball out of the hands of the women.

Fun and Games

Algonquian tribes had many different games they played. Some games were just for fun and included men and women, but others helped teach young boys the skills they needed to become good hunters and warriors. Common sports among Algonquian tribes included wrestling, foot races, lacrosse, jumping, hopping, throwing stones, and shooting arrows. They also played games similar to modern dice and card games, using bones and pieces of reeds. Some tribes played football games.

Besides learning the jobs of their mothers, young Algonquian girls also had some fun. Among other things, they learned how to make dolls out of corn husks, like the ones seen here.

Fate of the Algonquians

Most of the Algonquian Indians of New York were pushed out of the area early on by Iroquois warriors and European settlers. In fact, by the early 1700s, the Algonquian Indians in New York had been nearly wiped out by warfare and disease. Today there are only two Algonquian tribes with **reservations** in New York. Both are located on Long Island. The Poospatuck Reservation in Mastic, New York, is the home of the Unkechaga Nation. The Shinnecock Nation and Reservation is located in Southhampton, New York. Both tribes work to keep the **heritage** of their people alive.

Iroquois Confederacy

The **ancestors** of the Iroquois, or Haudenosaunee, moved into New York from the Pennsylvania region about 1,100 years ago. As they moved into the region, they pushed the Algonquian residents farther and farther east. Through the years, warfare was common between the Iroquois and Algonquians in the region. At first, fighting was also common among the Iroquois tribes themselves.

Great Law of Peace

According to Iroquois **tradition**, the fighting among themselves ended with the teachings of the ancient **prophets** Hiawatha and Deganawidah, the man known as the Great Peacemaker. The teachings convinced warring tribes to set aside their differences and follow the path of harmony and cooperation. This teaching was called the Great Law of Peace. The Iroquois stopped fighting one another and formed a powerful group known as the Iroquois **Confederacy**. This probably happened sometime around 1570.

Iroquois Confederacy

The Iroquois Confederacy was originally made up of five tribes, or nations. The sixth tribe, Tuscarora, became part of the Iroquois Confederacy in 1722. The following are the six nations of the Confederacy:

Cayuga (kay-you-gah)   **Onondaga** (on-on-dah-gah)
Mohawk (mo-hawk)   **Seneca** (seh-ni-kah)
Oneida (oh-ny-dah)   **Tuscarora** (tus-kah-roar-ah)

Organization

In the Iroquois Confederacy, each of the six nations had an equal voice in governing Iroquois territory and in settling arguments. There were nine clans within the Confederacy, with each nation having some or all of them. Members of the same clan were not allowed to marry. The Confederacy was run by a group of chiefs, or *sachem*, who were selected by their clan mothers. This group of leaders was called the Grand Council. Chiefs served for life, but clan mothers had the power to replace chiefs they felt were doing a bad job. In Iroquois society, the women owned all property (houses, farms, etc.) and were clan leaders. After marrying, a man moved into his wife's longhouse. Their children became members of the mother's clan.

Iroquois Clans

- Turtle
- Bear
- Wolf
- Heron
- Hawk
- Snipe
- Beaver
- Deer
- Eel

The headdresses worn by Iroquois men are called *gustowehs*. The *gustoweh* for each nation is different. You can tell them apart by the arrangement of the feathers.

Seneca   Cayuga   Onondaga

The Iroquois Grand Council dealt with foreign nations and people. It also settled arguments among the six nations, or **tribes**. The Iroquois Confederacy was divided into houses, or brotherhoods. The elder brothers were the Mohawks, Senecas, and Onondagas. The younger brothers were the Oneidas, Cayugas, and Tuscaroras. The Onondagas were known as the Firekeepers. Issues that come before the council were first considered by the elder brothers (Mohawks and Senecas), and then by the younger brothers (Oneidas, Cayugas, and Tuscaroras) as they met in the council. If these two sides were not able to reach an agreement, then the Onondagas cast the deciding vote. If the two sides came to an agreement, then the Onondagas had to agree to the decision as well in order to express unity within the Confederacy.

Iroquois Influence

The founding fathers of the United States were impressed with the way the Iroquois Confederacy governed itself. In the mid–1700s, colonial **delegates** traveled to Albany, New York, to meet with the Iroquois. An Onondaga named Canassatego suggested the English colonists form a union based on the Six Nations of the Iroquois Confederacy. His words impressed Benjamin Franklin, who published them in the 1740s. In 1754 the first colonial congress was held in Albany, and delegates from the Iroquois Confederacy attended. Some people think that later, in 1787, the writers of the Constitution of the new United States were partly influenced by the federal government of the Iroquois Confederacy.

Oneida

Mohawk

Tuscarora

Shelter

Iroquois villages were basically permanent. They were only moved if the area soil used for farming needed time to recover, which occurred about every 10 to 20 years. Some Iroquois villages were protected by a high **palisade**, with several longhouses inside.

Many Iroquois villages were protected by a tall, defensive wall of wooden poles, called a palisade. People could only enter the village through one narrow gateway, which could be easily defended.

Iroquois longhouses were made out of a frame of **saplings** bent into an arch and tied together to form a tunnel. That frame was then covered with overlapping layers of bark, usually from elm trees. There was a door at each end, and the roof had holes so the smoke from each of the fires could escape. Most longhouses were between 30 and 200 feet (9 and 61 meters) long, but they could be even longer. Several families of the same clan lived in each longhouse, with **partitions** separating each family. A common center aisle allowed the people to move freely through the longhouse. Long, braided husks of corn hung from the ceiling beams. Clothing, tools, toys, weapons, and dried foods were stored on shelves along the walls of the longhouse. There were also shelves with corn husk mats where the people slept.

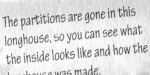

The partitions are gone in this longhouse, so you can see what the inside looks like and how the longhouse was made.

Confederacy of the Longhouse

The Iroquois Confederacy itself was set up like a 300-mile- (483-kilometer-) long longhouse, with one end at the Hudson River in the east and the other at Niagara Falls in the west. Members of the Mohawk Nation were the "Keepers of the Eastern Door" (near the Hudson River). Members of the Seneca Nation were the "Keepers of the Western Door" (near Niagara Falls). The Onondagas had the honor of tending the "central fire" since they were in the center of the region (see map on page 7). The central fire was kept in a longhouse.

Food

The need for food dominated the lives of most American Indians, and everyone played his or her part. The six Iroquois nations did more farming than many other American Indian nations. Women did most of the farming. They planted fields of corn, beans, and squash (also called the Three Sisters by the Iroquois) outside the protective walls of their villages. Corn was the most important crop, and corn soup was an important food. Corn was also used in Iroquois **ceremonies**. Different parts of the corn plant were used to make medicine, dolls, bandages, baskets, pipes, and sleeping mats. Women also planted pumpkins and sunflowers. Sunflower seeds were used to make oil and flour. Extra crops were dried and stored for both emergencies and the long, cold winters. The Iroquois made sure that nothing went to waste.

Strawberries

As with the Algonquian people, the Iroquois gathered ripe berries in the spring each year. Because strawberries are shaped like a heart, the Iroquois called them a food of spirit.

The leaves of strawberries were used to cure pains. Today, strawberries are still celebrated by the Iroquois with a special ceremony.

The Three Sisters

Corn, beans, and squash were planted in early summer. Seeds from all three were planted in small hills. The bean vines climbed the corn stalks, and the squash grew below. By midsummer, the fields looked overgrown with weeds but were actually filled with vegetables. The Iroquois called the three crops growing together the Three Sisters.

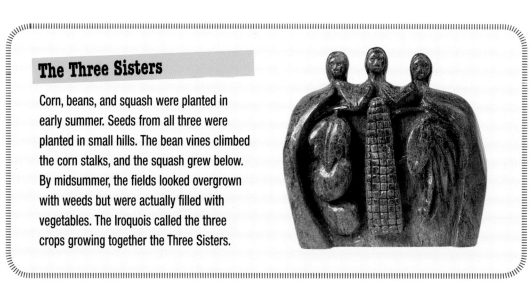

Iroquois women and children collected maple syrup from maple trees. They also gathered the same wild berries, nuts, and fruits as the Algonquian tribes of the area. What could not be eaten right away was dried and stored for the winter.

The main task of Iroquois men and older boys was to provide meat for the village by hunting and fishing. The bow and arrow was the weapon of choice for hunters and warriors. The Iroquois also used guns, once they could get them from Europeans. The Iroquois hunted deer, elk, rabbit, bear, moose, turkey, duck, and other animals found in the region. They hunted on foot, either alone or in groups. Most of the men of a village would go on a large hunt in the fall of every year. Sometimes they set large traps and led a herd of deer into them. The deer was the most important animal hunted. As with the Algonquian Indians, the Iroquois used every part of the deer. Hides were used for clothing, antlers and bones were used for tools, and of course the meat was eaten. Boys of a village could attend the hunt only after they had killed a deer by themselves to prove they were ready.

Snowshoes like this allowed Iroquois hunters to move quickly without sinking deep into the snow while tracking animals. Snow was sometimes helpful to the hunters, because it made animals easier to track and slowed down larger animals.

The Iroquois were experts at fishing the lakes, rivers, and streams of New York. They used the bow and arrow, spears, hooks, and nets when fishing. They sometimes fished from their dugout or elm bark canoes. The spring season was especially good for fishing. Just like the Algonquian people, groups of Iroquois took advantage of the large numbers of fish such as shad and salmon that **migrated** up New York's rivers each spring to deposit their eggs. The Iroquois used nets and traps to catch hundreds of fish at a time. They also collected shellfish for food and to be used as decoration.

Clothing and Accessories

Iroquois warriors wore their hair in a scalp lock, similar to the hairstyle we call a mohawk today. The men carefully shaved off all their facial and body hair. Iroquois women wore their hair long. Tattoos were common for men.

Iroquois clothing was made from **tanned** deer hide called **buckskin**. Women and girls wore long skirts or dresses, and often vests or shirts. Men and boys wore a kind of short skirt called a **breechcloth**. Both men and women often wore buckskin leggings to protect their legs while walking in the woods or tall grasses. Everyone wore moccasins. In warm weather, young children usually wore nothing at all. In the winter, the Iroquois wore capes or cloaks made from animal fur, often rabbit fur, to keep warm.

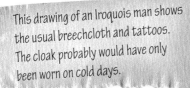

This drawing of an Iroquois man shows the usual breechcloth and tattoos. The cloak probably would have only been worn on cold days.

The Iroquois decorated their clothing and shoes with beads and dyed porcupine **quills**. Men sometimes wore porcupine quills or feathers in their locks of hair. The Iroquois also dyed moose hair blue, red, or yellow and used it to decorate clothing. Jewelry made from shells, beads, and other items was common for both men and women.

Religion and Ritual

The Iroquois believe in the Great Spirit, who they think created the world. They also believe there are other good and evil spirits. Many Iroquois ceremonies either give thanks to good spirits or attempt to scare away evil spirits. The Iroquois feel that evil spirits cause sickness and a poor harvest of crops.

A group of Iroquois called the False Face Society help to heal sickness and protect against evil spirits. They cut wooden masks called False Face Masks from living trees and decorated them. No two masks look the same. They also make masks called Husk Face Masks from corn husks. Members of the False Face Society wear the masks to scare away evil spirits. The masks are considered **sacred** objects, and the Iroquois believe they should only be seen by other members of the Iroquois nations.

The Iroquois held six large festivals every year, each of which usually lasted several days. They were held to give thanks to the good spirits for providing good health, clothing, a good harvest, and the happiness of the Iroquois people. Sacred tobacco was burned at the festival ceremonies. There were also speeches, prayers, music, dances, games, and a feast.

Like all American Indian nations, the Iroquois have a story of how the world was created. A long time ago, the world was only water, with the Sky World above it. A great *sachem*, or chief, in the Sky World took a tree out of the ground and his daughter, Sky Woman, fell through the hole. Swans flew under Sky Woman and slowed her fall with their wings. The animals in the water saw Sky Woman falling. They knew she could not swim, so they decided to create land for her. Muskrat took mud up from the bottom of the sea and put it on Turtle's back to create land. The swans put Sky Woman on Turtle Island (North America), where she walked in a circle dropping seeds she had brought from the Sky World. The seeds grew into the Three Sisters and all the other plants of the world.

Iroquois Festivals

Midwinter or New Year's Festival	early February	Celebrated the beginning of a new year. A long speech called the Thanksgiving Address was given at this seven-day festival.
Maple Festival	early spring	Gave thanks for the return of spring and to the maple tree for its sweet syrup.
Planting Festival	late spring	Gave thanks for the return of the planting season and asked good spirits to bless the seeds.
Strawberry Festival	early June	Celebrated the return of the first fruits of the earth after the long winter.
Green Corn Festival	August	Gave thanks to the good spirits who provided the crops now becoming ripe.
Harvest Festival	early October	Celebrated and gave thanks for the crops now being harvested, cooked, and stored for winter.

Iroquois artist Ernest Smith made this painting showing the Iroquois story of the creation of the world.

Modern lacrosse comes from Indian stickball. This 1867 photograph shows an Iroquois lacrosse team with their rackets.

Fun and Games

The Iroquois played a game of stickball as part of religious ceremonies. Two teams made up of hundreds of men played the game. One game could cover an area 20 miles (32 kilometers) long and could last many days. Players used wooden rackets and a ball made from deerskin or wood. It was a rough game, and sometimes players were hurt. The Iroquois liked to bet on which team would win.

Younger Iroquois entertained themselves in the winter by playing a game called snowsnake. They dragged a log through the snow to make a long, narrow path and then sprinkled the path with water to create a frozen track. The "snakes" were actually long, straight sticks from hickory branches. Players stood at the end of the track and slid the "snakes" up the track. The person who could slide the snake the farthest on the track was the winner. The Iroquois played many other games as well. Some were as simple as throwing hatchets or racing. Many games helped to teach young boys the skills they would need when they became hunters and warriors.

Fate of the Iroquois

Disease and warfare brought on by European settlers killed or pushed away many Iroquois people through the years. Many Iroquois of the Mohawk and Cayuga Nations fled to Canada after the Revolutionary War. Some Oneida reestablished themselves in the state of Wisconsin. However, other Iroquois remained in New York. Today, the Iroquois population in New York has grown to more than 20,000, living both on and off **reservations**. There are currently nine recognized reservations of Iroquois nations in New York.

Wampum

The Iroquois and other American Indians of the northeast region of the United States made white and purple beads called *wampum*. They did this by cutting and drilling **whelk** and **quahog** shells. They then sewed the beads into *wampum* belts, which were often considered sacred to the Iroquois people. *Wampum* belts had woven symbols or pictures, which only certain people in the tribe knew how to read. The belts recorded agreements between the tribes of the Iroquois, as well as treaties between the Iroquois and European settlers. *Wampum* was also later used as a form of money when dealing with the white settlers.

For years, sacred *wampum* belts of the Iroquois were in the collection of the Museum of the American Indian. In 1988 Iroquois in New York and Canada celebrated when the museum returned 11 of those belts.

New York Indians and Colonial History

For hundreds of years, American Indians lived in villages throughout the New York region. They took care of the **environment** around them and only used what they needed. With the creation of the Iroquois **Confederacy** around 1570, their Algonquian enemies in New York suffered, since they could not challenge such a large, powerful, and organized group. By the early 1700s, the remaining Algonquians had been pushed into eastern New York, to the east bank of the Hudson River and what is now Manhattan and Long Island. They would quickly suffer another crushing blow when a new and powerful people, the Europeans, came to New York.

At first New York's native peoples traded with the Europeans and even helped them to learn about the land. However, relations between American Indians and Europeans began to turn sour once the Indians realized these new people meant to stay in their region and take advantage of the land. The Iroquois and Algonquians of New York then played an important role in the colonial history of New York and North America.

Early Contact, 1609–1753

In 1609 French explorer Samuel de Champlain led a French and Algonquian force against a party of Mohawk warriors in northeast New York. Champlain claimed that part of New York for France. This fighting began a long period of on-and-off war between the Iroquois on one side, and the French and their Indian **allies** (usually Algonquian) on the other.

Also in 1609, Henry Hudson sailed up the Hudson River (named in his honor) and claimed the territory covering much of what is now New York, New Jersey, Delaware, and part of Connecticut for the Netherlands. This claim allowed the Dutch to set up trading posts in New York in the 1620s along the Hudson River. A settlement called New Amsterdam was located where New York City is today.

The Dutch were mainly interested in obtaining as many furs as possible to ship home for sale, rather than colonizing. However, they did try to establish a small agricultural community to support the traders and merchants. The Dutch traded for furs with the Algonquians on Manhattan Island and the Mohawk Nation at Fort Orange (present-day Albany). The Mohawks knew the land very well and brought many furs for trade, so the Dutch provided them with guns for hunting. This increased the number of furs Mohawks brought to the Dutch and also created an important bond between the Iroquois Confederacy and these European residents. When the English moved into the New York region in the 1660s, the Iroquois simply continued their trade with the newly arrived English. They were used to dealing with Europeans.

This illustration shows Indians hunting beaver with guns provided by the Europeans. In order to trade furs with Europeans, New York Indians hunted and killed more animals than they could use for the first time in their history.

Manhattan Bargain?

The story goes that the Dutch purchased Manhattan Island from New York Algonquian Indians for an amount equal to 24 dollars. This sale probably did take place, but the details are not clear. Historians do know that the Dutch did not actually give the Indians money, but instead traded them goods worth a fairly large amount.

The Algonquian Indians likely thought that the Dutch were giving them a gift in exchange for the use of their land, for hunting and farming rights. It was not unusual for more than one tribe or village to use the same territory, especially among the Algonquians. For this reason, the same piece of land would be "sold" again and again. This was an idea the Dutch could not understand.

The Algonquians living in Manhattan and other areas of New York learned soon enough what the European settlers had in mind. Any Indian who chose to remain on land "sold" to the settlers was forced to live by their laws, which were often unfair and cruel.

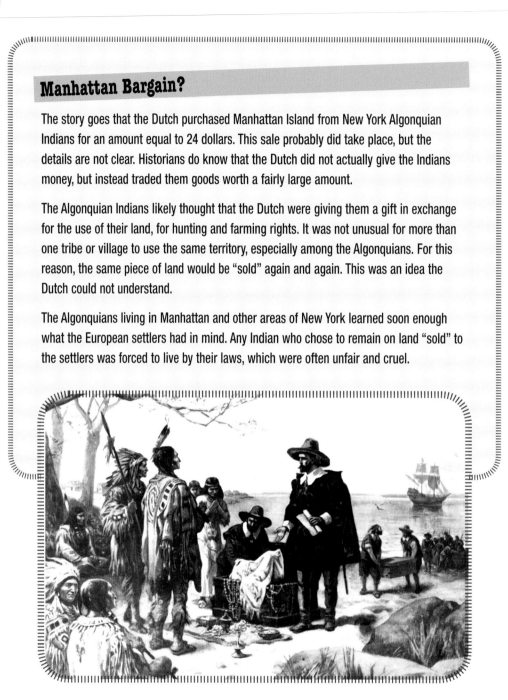

Many English colonists from Connecticut and Massachusetts settled on Long Island in the mid–1600s. They cooperated with the Dutch for a while, but in 1664, the English took control of New Amsterdam without a fight and named their colony New York. The English had control of southern New York, but the French were still interested in the northern part of the region.

French and Indian War, 1754–1763

In the early 1700s, the French began to build forts to secure their interests in New York. It was not long before fighting broke out between Great Britain and France, both in Europe and North America. The French and Indian War began in 1754. New York's Iroquoian and Algonquian Indians were caught in the middle of the fighting. They were usually forced to choose sides in the continuous fighting between the British and French.

The trading relationship that the Iroquois Confederacy had with the British kept the French out of the Hudson River valley. It also gave the British an advantage in trading and in the settlement of New York. The Iroquois also protected the "gateway" to the western frontier, which included the Ohio River valley. Settlers and traders had to go through the lands of the powerful Iroquois Confederacy to get to the western frontier. The Ohio River valley was very valuable for the fur trade. Both the French and British made claims of ownership of that land. The good relations the British had with the Iroquois gave them an advantage in settling the Ohio River valley. Iroquois attacks on western tribes also helped clear the land for English settlement.

The Fate of New York's Algonquians

As Europeans continued to come to New York, the majority of settlers moved into Algonquian lands. There were often fights between the Algonquians and European settlers. However, because the Algonquian nations were unorganized and often fought among themselves, they were unable to fight as a group against the colonists. Algonquians who were not driven from their land by guns usually died from European diseases, for which they had no resistance. By the early 1700s, the Algonquian Indian population in New York had been nearly wiped out.

The Iroquois Confederacy tried to stay officially **neutral** during the French and Indian War. But they remembered their bad experiences with Samuel de Champlain and the French. Because of that and their successful trade with the English in southern New York, the Iroquois tended to side with the British. The French found allies in the Algonquian tribes of the region. They also found an ally in the Huron Indians of Canada, who were a long-time enemy of the Iroquois Confederacy. The British finally won control of most of North America, including New York, when they defeated the French in 1763. It is unlikely that they could have beaten the French without the help of the Iroquois.

Cornplanter, a Seneca warrior, argued that the Iroquois Confederacy should stay out of the Revolutionary War, but the Seneca Nation chose to side with the British. After the Revolutionary War, Cornplanter became famous when he urged the Senecas to befriend the European settlers and accept their ways.

Abraham

In 1775 when many Iroquois were still choosing sides in the fight between the British and the colonists, a Mohawk named Abraham was selected to speak for the Iroquois Confederacy during a meeting with the **Continental Congress**. His explanation of Iroquois political theories greatly impressed and influenced the Americans. A single arrow can be easily snapped, he explained, but a dozen bound together cannot be broken. It was the Iroquois version of "united we stand, divided we fall."

Revolutionary War, 1775–1783

New York's American Indians again found themselves in the middle of a conflict when the colonists declared their independence from Great Britain. The two battled, and the American Revolutionary War began in 1775. The six nations of the Iroquois Confederacy were torn and did not want to choose sides in a war they did not want to fight. The Grand Council of the Confederacy met and officially declared themselves neutral in the war between Britain and the American colonists. However, there was no longer a strong sense of unity among the Iroquois nations at this time. The six nations had developed differences in **loyalties** and religion due to the influence of European settlers. Eventually, the Mohawks, Senecas, Cayugas, and Onondagas chose to side with their longtime British allies. The Oneidas and Tuscaroras supported the colonists.

Because most of the Iroquois sided with the British, American colonial forces invaded the lands of the Iroquois Confederacy in 1779. American forces burned Iroquois crops and villages, forcing the Indians to leave and scattering their population. Once the Americans defeated the British, most of the remaining Iroquois were driven from their lands. Even those who supported the new United States of America eventually lost their homes.

Joseph Brant was a Mohawk warrior who, along with his sister Mary, helped convince some members of the Iroquois Confederacy to side with the British in the Revolutionary War. In return, the British promised to return Mohawk lands. Brant was a fierce fighter known as Monster Brant by the colonists in the Mohawk Valley.

In 1784 many thousands of Iroquois fled to Canada. Those who chose to stay in New York were crowded onto **reservations**. The Revolutionary War really marked the end of Iroquois power in New York. Over the next 100 years, the Iroquois watched as their rights were ignored and their land was taken from them by white settlers and the State of New York.

Individual Iroquois continued to play important roles in the United States after the Revolutionary War. Ely Parker was a Seneca chief who was part of Ulysses S. Grant's staff during the Civil War (1861–1865). He was also the first American Indian appointed Commissioner of Indian Affairs.

Code of Handsome Lake

Perhaps the most important Iroquois leader in the years following the Revolutionary War was Ganeodiyo, a Seneca chief better known as Handsome Lake. During the 1790s, there were less than 5,000 Iroquois on reservations in New York. Alcohol and a lack of hope for the future were tearing this group apart. In 1799 Handsome Lake had a series of visions that he believed pointed to a path for his people to follow.

The Code of Handsome Lake combined parts of the Great Law of Peace with the religious beliefs of the peace-loving **Quakers**. It encouraged the social connections of family and community, and the importance of taking care of the land. It also forbade the consumption of alcohol. Handsome Lake's ideas became known as the "religion of the longhouse." He brought new pride and focus to the lives of many American Indians, not just the Iroquois. Many of New York's American Indians still follow the Code of Handsome Lake today.

New York Indians Today

Today, members of the six nations of the Iroquois **Confederacy** still live in the state of New York on several **reservations** and throughout the state. Two Algonquian tribes also have reservations on Long Island. People with Algonquian **heritage** live throughout New York. These American Indians work hard to preserve the land and **environment** of their reservations and the state of New York for present and future generations. They also have educational programs that pass on the knowledge of their long history and **traditions**.

There are currently about 60,000 American Indians living in the state of New York, with 14,000 of them living on reservations. About 40,000 American Indians live in New York City.

New York Reservations

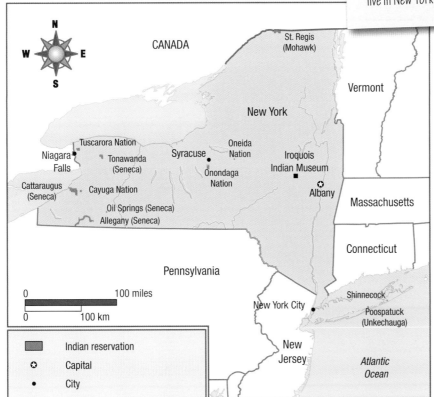

Iroquois Nations

The government of the six Iroquois nations and their reservations is based on the democratic principles of the Great Law of Peace that the Iroquois have worked with for hundreds of years. The Seneca Nation has four reservations in New York. They run the Seneca-Iroquois National Museum on the Allegany Indian Reservation, and two branches of the Seneca Nation Library. The museum often runs educational programs featuring Iroquois craftspeople demonstrating the traditional arts of bone and wood carving, beadwork, corn husk weaving, and more. The Seneca Nation also runs the Seneca Niagara Casino in Niagara Falls, New York. Today, about 500 people belong to the Cayuga Nation in New York, which is headquartered in western New York. They do not have a recognized reservation of their own, and most of their members live on or near the Allegany Reservation.

The Iroquois Indian Museum is located in Howes Cave, New York, near Albany. The museum is designed like a longhouse and has similar features. For instance, a skylight over the main gallery is similar to the smoke holes found in the roofs of Iroquois longhouses. The museum hosts a yearly Iroquois Indian Festival to celebrate traditional dress, crafts, and customs.

These Iroquois children are learning traditional dances of their **ancestors** at a yearly Iroquois festival in New York. With their help, the traditions of the Iroquois people will be preserved for future generations.

The Onondaga Nation has a reservation in central New York, where they have always lived. The Onondaga carry on their historic role as Keepers of the Central Fire of the Iroquois Confederacy. In 1838 most of the Oneida people moved to a reservation near Green Bay, Wisconsin. Some remained in New York, however, and the Oneida Nation here runs the Turning Stone Casino in Verona. The Tuscarora Indian school on the Tuscarora Reservation helps to preserve tribal **culture** by teaching students the Tuscarora language. The Tuscarora Reservation also holds the Tuscarora National Annual Picnic and Field Day in mid–July, as well as other events that celebrate the Tuscarora and Iroquois people.

The Mohawk Nation of New York runs the St. Regis Reservation on the New York-Canadian border. Many members of the Mohawk Nation found work in the construction of the skyscrapers and bridges in New York City and around the state. The largest manufacturer of lacrosse sticks in the United States and Canada is located on the St. Regis Reservation.

Indian Voices

American Indians of New York struggled to obtain equal rights and recognition from the federal government during the 1900s, and this fight continues today. A famous incident involved Wallace Anderson (middle right), a member of the Tuscarora Nation. After fighting in World War II (1939–1945) and the Korean War (1950–1953), Anderson held protests against the New York State Power Authority's takeover of some Tuscarora land. From that day on, he spent his life fighting for the rights of American Indians, often leading protests that made news headlines.

The 1960s and 1970s were a time when there was a great deal of Indian **activism** in the United States. Louis Bruce's father was a Mohawk, and Louis was raised among the Onondagas. In 1969 Bruce was named commissioner of the **Bureau of Indian Affairs** by President Richard Nixon. Bruce tried to bring American Indians into important positions within the bureau. This was an unpopular idea, and he was fired by Nixon in 1972.

The Onondaga Leon Shenandoah (right) was speaker of the Iroquois Confederacy from 1969 until his death in 1996. He worked for the return of Iroquois *wampum* belts from museums around New York. He also spoke to the United Nations twice and at the 1992 Earth Summit in Brazil. Shenandoah opposed **gambling** on Iroquois reservations, claiming that greed had no place in his people's culture.

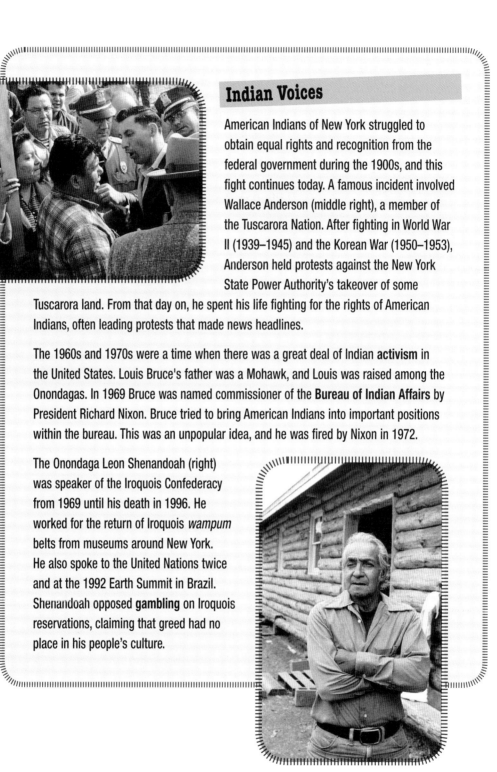

Algonquian Reservations

Today there are only two Algonquian tribes with reservations in New York, and they are both on Long Island. The Poospatuck Reservation in Mastic, New York, is the home of the Unkechaga Nation. The Shinnecock Nation and Reservation are located in Southhampton, New York. Both the Shinnecock and Unkechaga Nations were once part of the small Montauk Confederacy of Algonquian tribes on Long Island.

Long Island was one of the first places settled by the English. This led to the virtual destruction of the native cultures there. Because of this, the American Indians on Long Island have struggled to rediscover their language and traditions. Tribal members teach traditional dances and what language has been preserved. The Shinnecock Labor Day Weekend Powwow includes a day of traditional arts and crafts, foods, and dances.

American Indian Influence

It is impossible to have a clear picture of New York today without studying the many cultures that have lived here and influenced the state. The American Indians and their ancestors were the first people to live in New York. It is unlikely that the first European settlers could have survived and established successful colonies without the help of New York's native peoples.

Unfortunately, the Europeans who continued to come to New York did not return the favors of the Iroquois and Algonquian people. Despite years of broken treaties, land theft, and poor treatment, the American Indian cultures of New York have survived. We still benefit from their knowledge and traditions, and they continue to be an important part of New York's modern population.

Map of New York

N
W E
S

Plattsburgh
Lake Champlain
Lake Placid
Adirondack
Mountains
Ticonderoga
Watertown
Lake George
Lake Ontario
Oswego
Oneida Lake
Rome
Great
Sacandaga
Lake
Niagara Falls
Rochester
Syracuse
Utica
Buffalo
Seneca Falls
Mohawk River
Schenectady
Lake Erie
Canandaigua
Lake
Skaneateles Lake
Cooperstown
Albany
Dansville
Seneca
Lake
Cayuga Lake
Hudson River
Hudson
Ithaca
Finger Lakes
Nat'l Forest
Susquehanna River
Catskill
Mountains
Chautauqua Lake
Genessee River
Binghamton
Kingston
Poughkeepsie
White Plains
Montauk
New York City
Fire Island
National Seashore

0   50 miles
0   50 km

✪   capital
•   cities
⌇   river
▨   National Forest
▢   State Park
—   state line

CANADA
Maine
Vermont
New
Hampshire
New York
Massachusetts
Rhode Island
Connecticut
Ohio
Pennsylvania
New
Jersey
Atlantic
Ocean

Timeline

ca. 10,000 BCE
Paleo-Indians arrive in New York and become the first people to live there.

ca. 900 CE
Ancestors of the Iroquois (Haudenosaunee) move into New York from the southwest, pushing Algonquian peoples into eastern New York and Canada.

ca. 1570
The Cayuga, Mohawk, Oneida, Onondaga, and Seneca form the Iroquois **Confederacy**.

1609
Samuel de Champlain leads a French force against Iroquois in northeast New York.

Henry Hudson sails up Hudson River and claims territory for the Netherlands (Dutch).

1620s
Dutch traders set up posts along the Hudson River to trade with New York Indians for furs. The Dutch provide Mohawks with guns to use in the fur trade.

1626
According to a popular story, Dutch Governor Peter Minuit buys Manhattan Island from local Algonquian Indians for goods worth about 24 dollars.

1640s
English colonists from Connecticut and Massachusetts settle on Long Island.

1664
English take control of Dutch colony and rename it New York. New York Indians continue the fur trade with the English in place of the Dutch.

early 1700s
Algonquian people of New York nearly wiped out by warfare and disease by this time.

1722
The Tuscarora become the sixth nation of the Iroquois Confederacy.

1754
Iroquois delegates attend the first colonial congress in Albany, New York.

1754–1763
The French and Indian War is fought between the French and British. Most Iroquois side with the British, and most Algonquians side with the French. The British win with the help of the Iroquois, and the French are forced to leave North America.

1775
The Revolutionary War begins. The nations of the Iroquois Confederacy are divided, and the Mohawks, Senecas, Cayugas, and Onondagas side with the British, while the Oneidas and Tuscaroras support the colonists.

1779
American colonial forces invade Iroquois lands, burning villages and forcing them to leave the area.

1783
Colonial victory over Great Britain in Revolutionary War marks the end of the power of the Iroquois Confederacy.

1784
Many Iroquois **migrate** to Canada following the Revolutionary War.

1799
Seneca Chief Handsome Lake establishes the Code of Handsome Lake, also known as the religion of the longhouse, based on a series of visions he has.

1838
Most of the Oneida people of New York move to a **reservation** near Green Bay, Wisconsin.

1869
Ely Parker is the first Indian to be appointed Commissioner of Indian Affairs under President Ulysses S. Grant.

1969
Louis Bruce is named Commissioner of the **Bureau of Indian Affairs** and tries to raise American Indians to important positions within the Bureau. He is soon fired by President Richard Nixon.

1988
New York State Museum returns *wampum* belts to the Iroquois Confederacy.

2000
United States census shows 60,000 American Indians living in New York. Fourteen thousand of them live on reservations.

2004
United States government acknowledges that the Iroquois constitution influenced the U.S. constitution.

Glossary

activism practice that focuses on direct action in support of or opposition to an issue

afterlife existence after death

ally person or group of people who promise to help someone else

ancestor someone who came earlier in a family, especially earlier than a grandparent

archaeologist person who studies objects left behind by people who lived long ago

breechcloth small piece of clothing worn around the hips

buckskin strong, soft leather made from the skin of a deer

Bureau of Indian Affairs organization within the United States government that deals with the affairs and issues of American Indian nations and tribes

ca. stands for *circa*, meaning around

ceremony special act or acts done on special occasions

climate weather conditions in an area

confederacy group of peoples joined for some purpose

Continental Congress meeting of delegates from the American colonies that first met in Philadelphia, Pennsylvania, in 1774

cradleboard small wooden frame to which an infant is strapped

culture way of life of a group of people, including their food, clothing, shelter, and language

delegate person that a group sends to speak and act for it

descendant person who comes from a particular ancestor or family

elder person who has authority because of age and experience

environment surrounding objects and conditions that affect living things

extinct no longer living

fiber thread-like parts that form the tissue of plants and animals

forage search for something, such as food

gambling act of playing a game in which something, such as money, is risked for the chance of gain

herbs a plant used in medicine

heritage something handed down from the past or from one's ancestors

Ice Age period of time when a large part of the earth was covered with glaciers, which are huge sheets of moving ice

inherited received by right from a person at his or her death

jerky long, sun-dried slices of preserved meat

loyalty to be be faithful

mantle loose, sleeveless outer shirt

migrate move from one region to another, or pass from one region to another on a regular schedule

mussel shellfish with a soft body inside two shells hinged together

neutral not joining with either side in a quarrel, contest, or war

ocher red or yellow iron ore used for coloring

palisade fence made of large, pointed stakes to protect against attack

partition partial wall, panel, or other structure that divides or separates space

prophet religious leader who people believe speaks for a god or gods

quahog thick-shelled clam

Quaker popular name for a member of the Religious Society of Friends, which rejects war and stresses peace education

quill one of the sharp, stiff spines that stick out on the body of a porcupine; also a large, stiff feather from the wing or tail of a bird reed tall, thin grass found in wet areas

reservation land set aside by the government for American Indians

ritual established form for a ceremony or a system of rites

sacred holy, religious, or deserving respect and honor

sapling young tree

smoked exposed to smoke to keep from spoiling and give flavor; usually done with meat or fish

tanned made into leather, usually by soaking in a liquid in which something has been dissolved

tradition belief or custom handed down from one generation to another

tribe nation or group

vision quest ritual in which an American Indian tries to communicate with spirits by fasting (not eating) for a period of time

whelk large sea snail with a spiral shell

Find Out More

Further Reading

Dalton, Anne. *The Lenape of Pennsylvania, New Jersey, New York, Delaware, Wisconsin, Oklahoma, and Ontario.* New York: Rosen Publishing, 2005.

Englar, Mary. *The Iroquois: The Six Nations Confederacy.* Mankato, MN: Capstone Press, 2003.

McIntosh, Kenneth, and Marsha McIntosh. *Iroquois: North American Indians Today.* Broomall, PA: Mason Crest Publishers, 2003.

Mis, Melody S. *The Colony of New York: A Primary Source History.* New York: Rosen Publishing, 2007.

Yacowitz, Caryn. *Iroquois Indians.* Chicago: Heinemann Library, 2003.

Websites

http://www.iroquoismuseum.org/
This site, from the Iroquois Museum in Howes Park, New York, provides many links to finding out more information on this fascinating culture.

http://www.native-languages.org/york.htm
Learn more about New York's many native tribes at this informative site.

Index